Save OVER 50% OFF the cover pri

ACPL Laramie, WY
3910200003
Takanashi, M
Crimson hero
Pieces: 1
P9-BII-708

Six of the most addicti
Nana, Baby & Me, Absolute Boyfriend (by superstar creator Yuu Watase!!), and more! Plus the latest on what's happening in Japanese fashion, music, and culture!

Save 51% OFF the cover price PLUS enjoy all the benefits of the Sub Club with your paid subscription - your issues delivered first, exclusive access to ShojoBeat.com, and gifts mailed with some issues.

only $34.99 for 12 HUGE issues!

☑ YES! Please enter my 1-year subscription (12 GIANT issues) to *Shojo Beat* at the special subscription rate of only $34.99 and sign me up for the Sub Club.

NAME

ADDRESS

CITY STATE ZIP

E-MAIL ADDRESS P6BGNC

☐ MY CHECK, PAYABLE TO SHOJO BEAT, IS ENCLOSED

CREDIT CARD: ☐ VISA ☐ MASTERCARD

ACCOUNT # EXP. DATE

SIGNATURE

☐ BILL ME LATER PLEASE

CLIP AND MAIL TO

SHOJO BEAT
Subscriptions Service Dept.
P.O. Box 438
Mount Morris, IL 61054-0438

Canada add $12 US. No foreign orders. Allow 6-8 weeks for delivery.

Love. Laugh. Live

In addition to hundreds of pages of manga each month, ***Shojo Beat*** will bring you the latest in Japanes fashion, music, art, and culture—plus shopping, how-tos, industry updates, interviews, and much mor

DON'T YOU WANT TO HAVE THIS MUCH FUN

Only **$34.99** for **12 GIANT Issues!** **51% OFF** the Cover Price!

Shojo Beat
MANGA from the HEART
STRAIGHT FROM TOKYO: THE 10 DRINK MAGS
www.shojobeat.com
July 2005
WIN CASH PAGE 344
Godchild Absolute
www.shojobeat.com

NANA by AI YAZA

Subscribe Now! Fill out the coupon on the other side

Or go to: www.shojobeat.com

Or call toll-free 800-541-7876

by MITSUBA TAKANASHI | by TAEKO WATANABE | by MATSURI HINO | by MARIMO RAGAWA | by YUU WATAS

Absolute Boyfriend © 2003 Yuu WATASE/Shogakukan Inc. Akachan to Boku © Marimo Ragawa 1991/HAKUSENSHA, Inc. CRIMSON HERO © 2002 by Mitsuba Takanashi/SHUE
Kaze Hikaru © 1997 Taeko WATANABE/Shogakukan Inc. NANA © 1999 by Yazawa Manga Seisakusho/SHUEISHA Inc. Vampire Knight © Matsuri Hino 2004/HAKUSENSHA

FULL MOON WO SAGASHITE © 2001 by Arina Tanemura/SHUEISHA Inc.
Fushigi Yûgi: Genbu Kaiden © 2004 Yuu WATASE/Shogakukan Inc.
Ouran Koko Host Club © Bisco Hatori 2002/HAKUSENSHA, Inc.

Who needs enemies when you have a best friend like Mika?

Absolute Boyfriend™

by Yuu Watase

Only $8.99 EACH

Shojo Beat Manga

Absolute Boyfriend

Yuu Watase

2

Vol. 2 in stores August 1, 2006!

Absolute Boyfriend

1

Shojo Beat

MANGA from the HEART

THE REA DRAMA BE IN...

RATE

FOR OL TEE

On sale at:

www.shojobeat.com

Also available at your local bookstore and comic store.

Absolute Boyfriend
© 2003 Yuu WATASE/Shogakukan Inc.

viz media

Shojo Beat™
MANGA from the HEART

THE REAL DRAMA BEGINS IN...

A Celestial Warrior hides in the frozen north!

Only $8.99 EACH

Vol. 4 on sale now!

FUSHIGI YÛGI
GENBU KAIDEN™
By Yuu Watase

viz media

RATED T+ FOR OLDER TEEN

On sale at:
www.shojobeat.com
Also available at your local bookstore and comic store.

Fushigi Yûgi: Genbu Kaiden © 2004 Yuu WATASE/Shogakukan
Covers subject to change.

Shojo Beat
MANGA from the HEART
THE REAL DRAMA BEGINS IN...
When the dorms lose power, will love light the way?
Beauty is the Beast
By Tomo Matsumoto
Tomo Matsumoto
1
2
3
4
Only $8.99 EACH
On sale at:
www.shojobeat.com
Also available at your local bookstore and comic store.
In stores August 1, 2006!
viz media
Bijo ga Yaju © Tomo Matsumoto 2002/HAKUSENSHA, I
Covers subject to char

Shojo Beat
MANGA from the HEART
THE REAL DRAMA BEGINS IN...

Yuzuyu walks home from kindergarten by herself—and disappears!

Aishiteruze BABY★★™

By Yoko Maki

Only $8.99 EACH

In stores August 1, 2006!

On sale at:
www.shojobeat.com
Also available at your local bookstore and comic store.

AISHITERUZE BABY★★© 2002 by Yoko Maki/SHUEISHA Inc.
Covers subject to change.

Cain's troubled past pursues him through the grimy streets of 19th-century London!

Godchild

by Kaori Yuki

$8.99 each

Shojo Beat
THE REAL DRAMA BEGINS IN...
MANGA from the HEART

viz media
www.viz.com

SB
www.shojobeat.com

RATED T+ FOR OLDER TEEN

In stores August 1, 200

God Child © Kaori Yuki 2001/HAKUSENSHA, Inc.
Covers subject to change.

SB
The only thing standing in Kyoko's way are the two hottest guys in showbiz!
Series Debut!
Shojo Beat Manga
Skip·Beat!
Story & Art by
Yoshiki Nakamura
1
Only $8.99
Shojo Beat
THE REAL DRAMA BEGINS IN...
MANGA from the HEART
In stores July 4, 2006
www.shojobeat.com
Skip•Beat! © Yoshiki Nakamura 2002/HAKUSENSHA, inc.
RATED T for TEEN
viz media

CRIMSON HERO

VOL. 3
The Shojo Beat Manga Edition

This manga volume contains material that was originally published in English in *Shojo Beat* magazine, March–June 2006 issues.

STORY AND ART BY
MITSUBA TAKANASHI

Translation & English Adaptation/Naoko Amemiya
Touch-up Art & Lettering/Mark Griffin
Design/Courtney Utt
Editor/Nancy Thistlethwaite

Managing Editor/Megan Bates
Director of Production/Noboru Watanabe
Vice President of Publishing/Alvin Lu
Vice President & Editor in Chief/Yumi Hoashi
Sr. Director of Acquisitions/Rika Inouye
Vice President of Sales & Marketing/Liza Coppola
Publisher/Hyoe Narita

CRIMSON HERO © 2002 by Mitsuba Takanashi
All rights reserved. First published in Japan in 2002 by SHUEISHA Inc., Tokyo. English translation rights in the United States of America and Canada arranged by SHUEISHA Inc. Some scenes have been modified from the original Japanese edition. The stories, characters and incidents mentioned in this publication are entirely fictional.

The ASICS word and logo are trademarks owned by ASICS America Corporation.

No portion of this book may be reproduced or transmitted in any form or by any means without written permission from the copyright holders.

Printed in Canada

Published by VIZ Media, LLC
P.O. Box 77010
San Francisco, CA 94107

Shojo Beat Manga Edition
10 9 8 7 6 5 4 3 2 1
First printing, August 2006

www.viz.com store.viz.com

♥I'm so busy!! There's the drama CD, the magazine, the manga volumes, the storyboards, color pages, and research. I can't slack off on any of these things so it's a constant battle against time. No matter how much I do, it's not enough. And I want to work on other manga and do illustrations too. It'd be nice if there were one other me. If only I could self-replicate and morph into two. Then I could do more of the things I want to do.

—Mitsuba Takanashi, 2004

Mitsuba Takanashi debuted her first short story, *Mou Koi Nante Shinai* (Never Fall in Love Again), in 1992 in *Bessatsu Margaret* magazine and now has several major titles under her belt.

Born in the Shimane Prefecture of Japan, Takanashi now lives in Tokyo, where she enjoys taking walks, watching videos, shopping, and going to the hair salon. Takanashi has a soft spot for the Japanese pop acts Yellow Monkey and Hide, and is good at playing ping-pong.

THE WORLD CUP BEGINS IN NOVEMBER. I BET I'LL BE GLUED TO MY TV, ROOTING FOR THESE GIRLS WHO WILL REPRESENT JAPAN AS THEY TAKE ON THE WORLD.

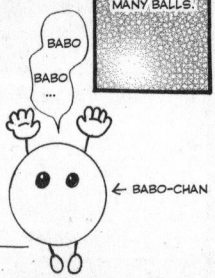

THIS ARTICLE APPEARED IN THE NOVEMBER 2003 ISSUE OF BETSUMA.

A PHOTO FROM THAT TIME →

HEH HEH

WASN'T THE WORLD CUP AMAZING?! ESPECIALLY THE GIRLS. I WENT TO YOYOGI TO SEE THE KOREAN MATCH AND I WAS REALLY IN TEARS!! YES I WAS.

I WISH THE ALL-JAPAN GIRLS AND BOYS THE BEST IN THEIR UPCOMING ENDEAVORS.

FEBRUARY 20, 2004
MITSUBA TAKANASHI

I FOLLOWED THEM TO THE MIYAZAKI TRAINING CAMP.
THEY WERE OYAMA AND KURIHARA.
THERE WERE TWO PLAYERS WHO JUST GRADUATED FROM THIS YEAR'S SPRING TOURNAMENT.
KANA OYAMA NUMBER 17. 187 CM. [ALMOST 6 FOOT 2] LEFT.
MEGUMI KURIHARA NUMBER 18. 186 CM. [OVER 6 FOOT 1] LEFT.
PEOPLE EXPECT THESE TWO TO BECOME THE NEW "FIGHTING POWER."
RIGHT BEFORE THE WORLD CUP! REPORT FROM MIYAZAKI: THE ALL-JAPAN GIRLS VOLLEYBALL TRAINING CAMP!!
MIYAZAKI IS THE TROPICS, I TELL YOU.
MIYAZAKI IS HOT HOT HOT...
A MANGA-KA WHO PLAYED VOLLEYBALL IN JUNIOR HIGH AND STILL PLAYS TO THIS DAY.
KANON OZAWA
OVER THERE IS KUMI NAKADA.
TAKANASHI WAS TRYING HARD TO LEARN SOMETHING BEFORE LEAVING.
KANON OZAWA WAS MOVED TO TEARS.
MMPH
TAKANASHI LOVED HER SMILE AND THE WAY SHE PLAYED. SHE USED TO ENERGIZE EVERYONE WATCHING HER.
WE WENT TO OBSERVE PRACTICE RIGHT AWAY, AND SAID OUR GREETINGS TO THE MANAGER.
HEY...THIS IS NONE OTHER THAN KAZUMI NAKAMURA. SHE'S THE FORMER ALL-JAPAN ATHLETE THAT WENT BY THE NICKNAME KYU-CHAN.
I USED TO READ BETSUMA [BESSATSU MARGARET] ALL THE TIME AS A STUDENT!
MY NAME'S NAKA-MURA.
I LIKE SMAP.
IT ENERGIZES ME TO LISTEN TO THEIR SONGS.
MISS OYAMA IS FROM SEITOKU GAKUEN OF TOKYO. SHE SAYS THAT WHEN SHE'S NOT PRACTICING, SHE LEADS A NORMAL HIGH SCHOOL LIFE LIKE EVERYONE ELSE.
AT LAST YEAR'S HIGH SCHOOL SPRING VOLLEYBALL TOURNAMENT, THEY PLAYED AGAINST EACH OTHER. EACH WAS THE ACE PLAYER ON HER TEAM.
I USED TO READ THE DEVIL DOES EXIST.
IT WAS POPULAR IN THE DORMS. WE'D READ THEM AND PASS THEM AROUND.
THEY BOTH LIKE WINNIE THE POOH.
MISS KURIHARA IS FROM MITAJIRI GIRLS SCHOOL OF YAMAGUCHI PREFECTURE. SHE SAYS THAT SHE LIVED IN A DORM IN HIGH SCHOOL AND DID NOTHING BUT VOLLEYBALL.
WE WERE TO INTERVIEW BOTH ATHLETES, OYAMA AND KURIHARA, AFTER DINNER.
THEY BOTH STILL HAD A GIRLISH INNOCENCE ABOUT THEM.
A!
B!
THE SETTER, TAKESHITA, IS SO COOL!
HER TOSSES ARE SO ACCURATE.
THEY GO EXACTLY WHERE THE ATTACKER REQUESTS.
AFTER THIS, WE WENT TO OBSERVE A PRACTICE GAME AGAINST MIYAKONOJOU HIGH SCHOOL'S BOYS' VOLLEYBALL TEAM. THEY WERE IN THE SPRING TOURNAMENT.
WOW!
THEY'RE LIKE A MACHINE.
AMAZING!!
THIS IS JAPAN AT ITS BEST!

Crimson
Hero

ANY TEAM THAT LOSES A PRACTICE GAME TO SHOEI...
...IS CERTAINLY NO MATCH FOR US.
THE INTER-HIGH PRELIMS LOOMED CLOSER...
...AS WE ENTERED INTO SUMMER.
TO BE CONTINUED...

YOU'RE NO LONGER THE TOMOYO OSAKA I USED TO ADMIRE.
HAYASHIDA FROM YABESHO HIGH!
SO WE MEET AGAIN.
COME TO THINK OF IT, WE LIVE NEAR EACH OTHER, DON'T WE?
I HAD NO DESIRE TO RUN INTO YOU, BELIEVE ME.
...
THAT'S RIGHT! IS THAT A PROBLEM?
NO... NOT AT ALL.
IT'S JUST THAT...
I HEARD YOU STARTED PLAYING VOLLEYBALL AGAIN.

VOOSH
RUMBLE
RUMBLE
OH!
5
B-DMP

...HURT FAR TOO MUCH.
...MY HEART...

THE SOUND OF HIS VOICE...
...AND THE WAY HE GRABBED MY SHOULDER... I DIDN'T KNOW WHAT TO MAKE OF IT.
BUT FOR MERE CURIOSITY...
asics

THIS IS JUST...
...CURIOSITY. THAT'S ALL.
...
NOBARA...!
HAIBUKI SHOUTED.

!
WHAT ARE YOU DOING...?
...
I THOUGHT YOU DIDN'T *LIKE* HIM LIKE THAT.
RIGHT?
YU...
I HEARD SHE'S HERE, SO...
YUSHIN'S GIRLFRIEND.

asics
...FROM JEALOUSY.

I DON'T WANT TO SEE YOU GET HURT.
...OR SUFFER...
ALL RIGHT!
OOPS. GOTTA RUN.

OH!
GUESS WHAT HAPPENED, NOBARA!
PSST
WHAT?
WHOA! HEY, TOMONORI.
YOU STARTLED ME.
YUSHIN'S GIRLFRIEND IS HERE!
...HUH?
APPARENTLY SHE WAS IN THE AREA SO SHE DROPPED BY TO WATCH HIM PRACTICE.
SHE'S OUTSIDE RIGHT NOW.
SHUFF
SHUFF
HEY, FIRST-YEAR! BRING THE BALLS AFTER YOU'VE FINISHED YOUR WARM-UP.

THERE'S THE INTER-HIGH PRELIMS...
...AND THEN I RETIRE.
NOBARA'S WORKING HARD.
...
GIRLS RESTRO
KCHAK

WBBL
AAAAARGH! IT'S KILLING ME!
I CAN'T GO ON.
...LET'S TAKE A BREAK.
HUF
NOBARA'S NOT BACK FROM THE BATHROOM YET.
IT'S OKAY. SHE'S JUST THROWING UP.
THAT GIRL DOESN'T STOP JUMPING 'TIL SHE THROWS UP.
asics

THE DORM WILL BE DESTROYED!!
I DON'T UNDER-STAND.
WHAT DOES IT MEAN TO LIKE SOMEONE?
AAAAAAGH!?

THUMP
THUMP
I'M SORRY, I'M SORRY. I WON'T DO IT AGAIN!
HOW DARE YOU PUT SOMEONE ON DISPLAY FOR YOUR OWN AMUSEMENT!!
UNBELIEVABLE!
...
NOBARA, YOU OKAY?
VWOOSH
WAIT! WAIT, YUSHIN! CALM D--
BOKK
AGH!
...
NOBARA ?
NOBA...
THAT FRICKIN' HURT...!

SLAM
AGH!
I KEPT HEARING ALL THIS SHOUTING AND NOISE, AND NOW I KNOW WHY!
NAOTO! YOU ROTTEN LITTLE...
GLARE

HEY, DO YOU HAVE A PICTURE OF HIS GIRL-FRIEND?
SFF
SFF
SFF
HERE!
I SHOULD.
IT'S SOMEWHERE AROUND HERE.

...BEFORE TELLING HIS CURRENT GIRLFRIEND HOW HE FELT ABOUT HER.
SHE WAS THE TEAM MANAGER, SEE.
I DON'T WANT TO CAUSE TROUBLE FOR ANYONE.
BESIDES, I DON'T WANT TO BE THINKING ABOUT HER IN THAT WAY DURING PRACTICES.
HE ACTED SO COOL ABOUT IT.
OF COURSE, IT WAS TOTALLY OBVIOUS THAT THEY BOTH LIKED EACH OTHER.
IT WAS FRUSTRATING TO WATCH!
HA HA. YEAH, YUSHIN ALWAYS ACTS LIKE SOME TOUGH GUY.
OH YEAH? THAT'S SO LIKE HIM.

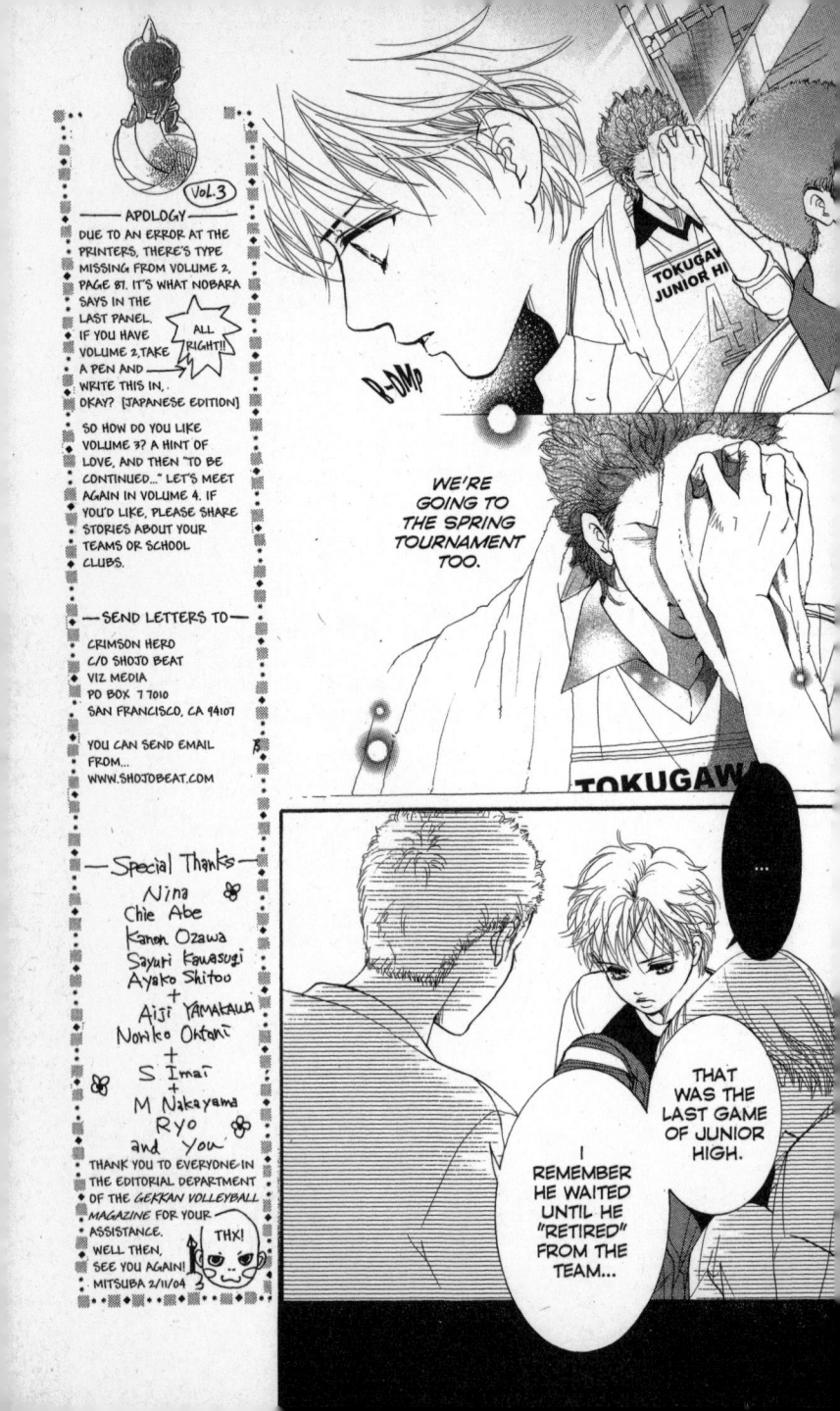

Vol.3

— APOLOGY —

DUE TO AN ERROR AT THE PRINTERS, THERE'S TYPE MISSING FROM VOLUME 2, PAGE 81. IT'S WHAT NOBARA SAYS IN THE LAST PANEL. IF YOU HAVE VOLUME 2, TAKE A PEN AND WRITE THIS IN, OKAY? [JAPANESE EDITION]

ALL RIGHT!!

SO HOW DO YOU LIKE VOLUME 3? A HINT OF LOVE, AND THEN "TO BE CONTINUED..." LET'S MEET AGAIN IN VOLUME 4. IF YOU'D LIKE, PLEASE SHARE STORIES ABOUT YOUR TEAMS OR SCHOOL CLUBS.

— SEND LETTERS TO —

CRIMSON HERO
C/O SHOJO BEAT
VIZ MEDIA
PO BOX 7010
SAN FRANCISCO, CA 94107

YOU CAN SEND EMAIL FROM...
WWW.SHOJOBEAT.COM

— Special Thanks —

Nina
Chie Abe
Karen Ozawa
Sayuri Kawasugi
Ayako Shitou
+
Aiji YAMAKAWA
Noriko Ohtani
+
S Imai
+
M Nakayama
Ryo
and You

THANK YOU TO EVERYONE IN THE EDITORIAL DEPARTMENT OF THE *GEKKAN VOLLEYBALL MAGAZINE* FOR YOUR ASSISTANCE.

THX!

WELL THEN, SEE YOU AGAIN!
MITSUBA 2/11/04

BWAAAAH!
YOU'D BETTER NOT TELL YUSHIN, THOUGH.
I'M SERIOUS. HE'D KILL ME FOR SURE.
FINE, I WON'T. ARE THE PICTURES THAT STRANGE?
YOU BETTER NOT BREATHE A WORD, OKAY?
WHAT WERE YOU GUYS DOING?
NO WAY!
AAAH HA HA HA!
HE SAID THEY WERE ON AN OVERNIGHT FROM SCHOOL.
A CAT PRINCE!
HA HA HA.
I CAN'T BELIEVE YOU TOOK PHOTOS AFTER LOSING.
THAT ONE'S RIGHT AFTER LOSING A GAME.

...
HA HA!
AGH. IT'S NOBARA.
HEY! C'MON, NAOTO.
BANG BANG
YOU'RE SUPPOSED TO PUT AWAY YOUR OWN LAUNDRY!
HOW MANY TIMES DO I HAVE TO TELL YOU?
206 TSUCHIYA
SO WHAT? LET HER SEE THIS STUFF TOO!
KCHAK
206 TSUCHIYA
HEY---
SHHH. BE QUIET.
?
PHOTO ALBUMS FROM JUNIOR HIGH?
YEAH, YEAH. I WANT TO SEE THEM!

SO BASICALLY...
PINK
...HE'S SAYING THAT IF I FALL FOR YUSHIN...
...I'LL BE REJECTED...
...AND END UP BEING JEALOUS OF HIS GIRLFRIEND.
...
BUT I ALREADY SAID I DON'T LIKE HIM LIKE THAT!
WHOMP
HOW STUPID!
!

NOBARA, YOU WERE THE GREATEST.
YOU'RE THE BEST.
...BUT I WANT YOU TO BE NUMBER ONE, JUST LIKE YOU ALWAYS USED TO BE.
OH.
...THAT'S ALL.

I DON'T WANT TO SEE YOU GET HURT...
...OR SUFFER FROM JEALOUSY.
I DON'T WANT THOSE THINGS TO HAPPEN TO YOU.
I KNOW IT'S SELFISH OF ME...

WELL, I TRUST HIM, AND THINK HE'S A GOOD GUY AND ALL.
...
BUT THAT'S NOT THE SAME THING AS LIKING HIM!!
NOT THAT I REALLY EVEN KNOW WHAT THAT MEANS.
LIKE, LOVE, WHATEVER!!
I DON'T WANT TO SEE YOU GET REJECTED.
B-DMP

I ASKED YOU IF YOU LIKE YUSHIN? DO YOU HAVE A THING FOR HIM?
WHY...?
WHERE DID THAT COME FROM?
NO, OF COURSE NOT.
NO, OF COURSE NOT.
DID YOU HEAR ME? I SAID IT TWICE.
YOU SURE?

5-1
SHE'LL BE THE BEST.
BECAUSE I CAN COUNT ON NOBARA.
SHE WILL ALWAYS DO IT FOR ME.
...IT'S OKAY THAT I CAN'T RUN.
...HUH?

GRADE 5 ROOM 1
IT'S A MARATHON.
EVERYONE IS RUNNING IN P.E. RIGHT NOW!
REALLY? I'LL WATCH WITH YOU.
TEACHER!
SHE'S NUMBER ONE ON THE BARS ...
...AND IN VOLLEYBALL AND SOCCER AND EVERY-THING!!
IT'S SO LIKE HER TO BE THE BEST.
NOBARA'S THE BEST. SEE?
SHE'S WAY FASTER THAN ANY OF THE BOYS.
DON'T WORRY.
YOU'LL BE STRONG ENOUGH TO RUN LIKE THAT IN NO TIME.

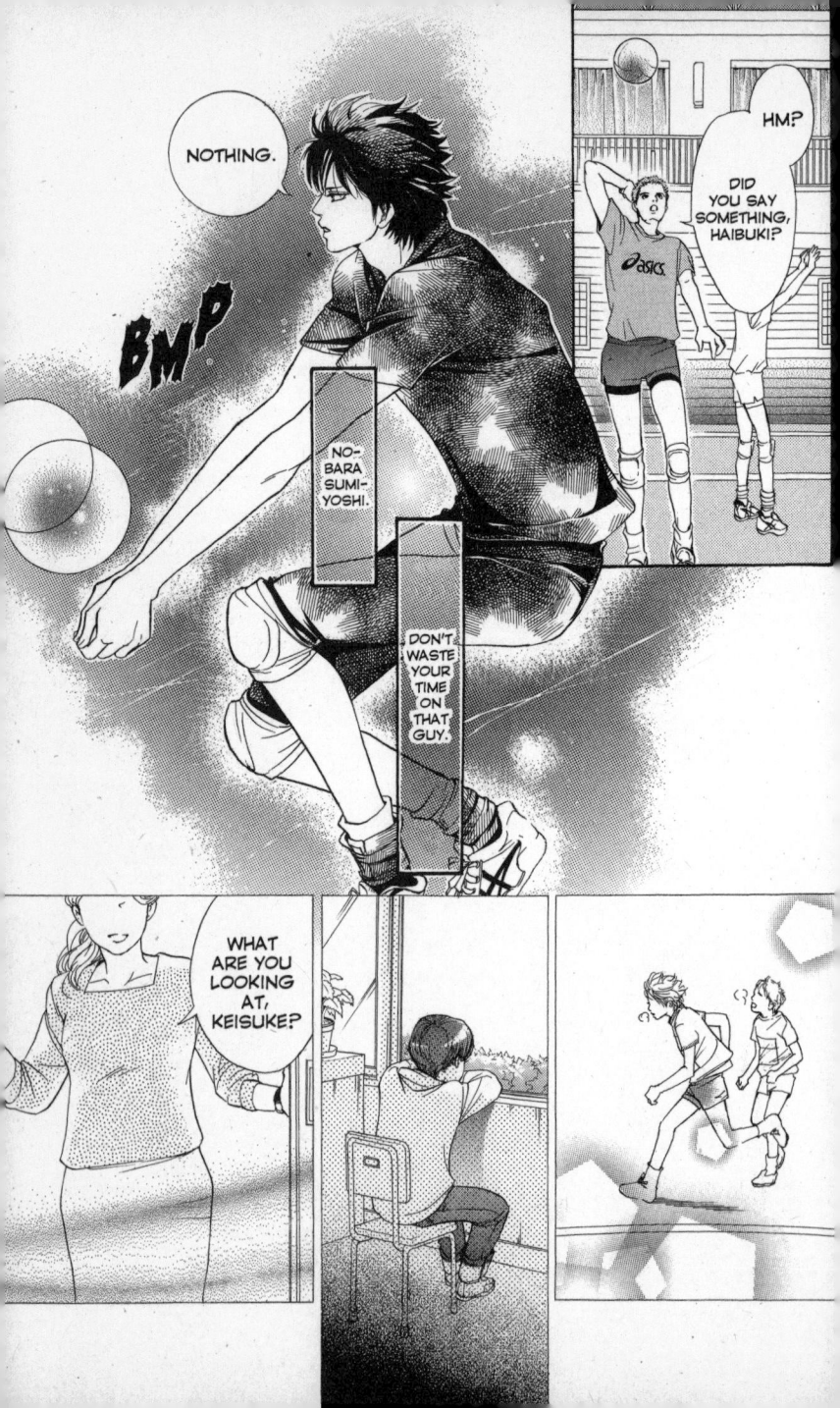
HM?
DID YOU SAY SOMETHING, HAIBUKI?
NOTHING.
BMP
NO-BARA SUMI-YOSHI.
DON'T WASTE YOUR TIME ON THAT GUY.
WHAT ARE YOU LOOKING AT, KEISUKE?

...AT LEAST NOW WE'RE ALLOWED TO HAVE THAT DREAM.
IT'S OUR RIGHT.
AM I GONNA HAVE TO SPELL IT OUT?
asics
WE HAVE FREE-DOM...
...TO DREAM.

I MEAN, WE'RE GOING TO THE SPRING TOURNAMENT TOO.
HEY, VOLLEYBALL RECRUIT! GET TO YOUR POSITION NOW!
YES!
EVEN IF IT'S A DREAM WITH A ONE-IN-A-MILLION CHANCE...

HE'S PART OF THE ELITE TOO.
B-BMP
WH-WHAT?
NO, I DON'T THINK IT'S FUNNY.
YOU THINK IT'S FUNNY THAT I WANT TO MAKE IT TO THE SPRING TOURNA-MENT?!

YOU WOULD ASK?
BY THE WAY, WHAT IS OUR RANK RIGHT NOW?
BUT OUT OF ABOUT 250 SCHOOLS HERE IN TOKYO...
...ONLY THE TOP THREE TEAMS FROM THE PRELIMINARIES GET TO PARTICIPATE!
IGNORE THE FOOLS. LET'S PRACTICE.
HA HA HA
BLEH!
BOTTOM OF THE HEAP, BAR NONE!
IN THE CASE OF GIRLS VOLLEYBALL, IT'S AN ESPECIALLY FIERCE BATTLE. ONLY THE RENOWNED SCHOOLS EVER MAKE IT.
OOH!
HMPH! SO WHAT?
THAT'S WHAT I HATE ABOUT THE ELITE.

YOU THINK BEING ABLE TO DO CROSS-OVERS IS ENOUGH TO GET YOU TO THE SPRING TOURNAMENT?!
HA HA HA! I SPOT A FOOL ON THE GIRLS' TEAM!!
DUMMY!
TOMOYO, WHAT'S THE SPRING TOURNAMENT?
SHUT UP. WE WILL TOO GO TO THE SPRING TOURNAMENT!
STRENGTHENING ARMS WITH RUBBER EXERCISE BANDS
YES! ONE STEP CLOSER TO THE SPRING TOURNAMENT!
GUTS!!!
THUD
IT'S THE NATIONAL CHAMPION-SHIPS HELD IN THE SPRING!
...DREAMS OF PLAYING ON THE ORANGE COURTS OF THE YOYOGI GYM.
ACROSS THE NATION, EVERYONE WHO PLAYS HIGH SCHOOL VOLLEYBALL...
THERE ARE ORANGE COURTS.

DASH!
A CROSSOVER!* SINCE WHEN COULD SHE DO THAT?!
MY DREAM ...
SHE'S ALREADY DONE IT 50 TIMES TODAY.
F-FIFTY?!
*A MOVING ATTACK THAT FLOWS FROM THE CENTER TO THE RIGHT. IT REQUIRES A GREAT EXERTION OF ENERGY FROM THE ATTACKER.
HUFF
IT'S IN.
SILENCE
BAM

FOR TWO AND A HALF YEARS...
...I GET TO DEVOTE MYSELF TO VOLLEYBALL. I HAVE NO REGRETS.
YOU'RE THE PLAYBOY...!
AAGH!!
TMP TMP
WHAT?!
I'LL GET YOU, HAIBUKI! WHAT DOES IT SAY?!
PLAYBOY
HA HA HA!
CAPTAIN!!
THE GIRLS ARE DOING SOME KIND OF INTENSIVE DRILL, AND THEY'RE MONOPOLIZING THE WHOLE COURT!
WHAT?
WE'VE GOT A PROBLEM!
YO!
SO WHAT IS IT?!
I'M PISSED OFF.
WE'VE GOT A PROBLEM, CAPTAIN!
WHAT?
I TOLD YOU TO GET THE NET UP AND START YOUR COMBINATION DRILLS.

AND YUSHIN ISN'T THE ONLY ONE.
BECAUSE OF YUI, AYAKO, AND THE OTHERS...
...I HAVE THE STRENGTH TO KEEP TRYING.
LOOKS LIKE IT.
SHE CAN PLAY VOLLEYBALL FOR ONLY TWO AND A HALF MORE YEARS, HUH?
YEAH? SO THEY'LL SUPPORT HER UNTIL SHE GRADUATES?
GUESS SO.
PAT

SO I--
HA
OK. I GOT IT. RELAX.
HE...
...UNDERSTANDS ME.
!
STU
THE REAL AU

OH!
WHA--!
HEY! NO!
WHADDYA TALKIN' ABOUT?!
YOU THINK...
HEY!
DON'T GET THE WRONG IDEA!!
IDIOT!
DESPERATE
I KNOW YOU HAVE A GIRLFRIEND.
AND UM...
I JUST... I'M SORRY. I'M OBLIVIOUS TO THIS KIND OF THING.
THAT HURT!
IT'S NOT LIKE THAT! YOU JUST...
...HAPPENED TO BE STANDING THERE LIKE A TELEPHONE POLE!
TELEPHONE POLE? FIRST A TOWEL, NOW A TELEPHONE POLE?
BUT THE THING IS... I THINK OF YOU AS A FRIEND I CAN TRUST!

I'LL WASH IT. SORRY.
DON'T USE MY SHIRT FOR THAT!!
...
FORGET ABOUT THE SHIRT. BUT LISTEN...
OOPS. SORRY, I MISTOOK IT FOR A BIG TOWEL.
A TOWEL?!
I'M HAPPY TO LISTEN TO YOU AND STUFF...
...BUT DON'T CLING TO ME, OKAY?
I MEAN, YOU ARE A GIRL, YOU KNOW.

I'M GOING TO WORK SO HARD...
SNIFF
SNIFF
!!

HUH? WHAT'S... UH... NOBARA?!
SHE SAID... I CAN PLAY VOLLEYBALL!
VOLLEYBALL IS AS IMPORTANT TO ME AS MY FAMILY.
SHE ACCEPTED THAT...
FINALLY.

SET 12

SILENT LOVE

SON DORM

!
HEY! SO HOW WAS YOUR VISIT HOME?

...
NOW GO!
YOU'LL MISS THE LAST TRAIN.
PAT
HAKONE
RRRRRRRING
NOVA SAVINGS
PACIFIC BANK

IT'S OKAY. KEEP IT, DAD!
YOU ONLY GET A SMALL ALLOWANCE FROM MOTHER.* YOU CAN'T—
IT'S ONLY A LITTLE.
JUST BE QUIET AND TAKE IT!
*IN JAPAN, THE WIFE CONTROLS THE FAMILY BUDGET.
I WISH I COULD DO MORE FOR YOU.
AT LEAST LET ME LOOK GOOD ONCE IN A WHILE.

THEN I'LL DO MY BEST AS WELL.
DAD!
YEAH. GETTING SUPPLIES.
STILL WORKING?
TAKE THIS.
PACIFIC BANK
SAVINGS PASSBOOK
NOBARA SUMIYOSHI
A LITTLE PARTING GIFT FROM ME!
NOBARA.
NOBARA!

MOTHER, IF YOU COULD ONLY HAVE SEEN NOBARA PLAY!
SHE LOOKED SO HAPPY PLAYING VOLLEYBALL!
...SOUKA...
YES.
SO... IS THAT A PROMISE FROM THE BOTH OF YOU?

I'LL WORK HARD TO BE A WORTHY SUCCES-SOR.
BUT I WANT YOU TO WAIT.
PLEASE. DURING MY THREE YEARS IN HIGH SCHOOL...
...
...I WANT TO PLAY VOLLEYBALL!
OH PLEASE, MOTHER!
I'LL HELP OUT WITH SEIRYU DURING THAT TIME.
FOR THREE YEARS...
...LET ME LIVE MY OWN LIFE.

...
I'LL DO IT. I'LL CARRY SEIRYU ON.

VOLLEYBALL HAS NOTHING TO DO WITH THIS!
DON'T RAISE YOUR VOICE AT YOUR GRAND-MOTHER!
JUST BE QUIET FOR A MOMENT.
...
FORGET IT. I DON'T KNOW WHY I EVEN CARE ANYMORE.

AND YOU'RE NO DIFFERENT, MOTHER!
THAT JERK TALKED ABOUT SOUKA LIKE SHE WAS AN OBJECT.
HE ASSUMED SHE'D OBEY HIS EVERY COMMAND!
MY, WHAT A FRIGHT!
SHOUTING IN THE MIDDLE OF THE NIGHT, INDEED!
GRAND-MOTHER.
YOU THINK WE SHOULD HAVE NO WILL OF OUR OWN!
YOU USE US LIKE PAWNS!
SHE WOULDN'T HAVE TURNED OUT TO BE SUCH A ROUGH CHILD IF YOU HADN'T LET HER CONTINUE VOLLEYBALL.

DO YOU INTEND TO BRING SEIRYU TO RUIN?!
IS THAT IT, MISS NOBARA?!
MOTHER, WAIT.
SHE WAS JUST COMING TO MY RESCUE.
YOU STAY QUIET!
THERE SHE GOES AGAIN, IGNORING OUR SIDE OF THE STORY.
IF YOU NEED TO SAY NO, A SIMPLE EXPLANATION WOULD HAVE BEEN SUFFICIENT.
TO THINK THAT YOU INJURED HIM!
DO YOU HAVE ANY IDEA HOW MUCH I HAD TO APOLOGIZE TO MR. YOKOTA?
DO YOU HAVE ANY IDEA?! NOBARA!
I DID NOTHING WRONG.

JUST ARRIVED
AUNT MOMOKO!
FOOD? ♡
NO!
!
MY SISTER IS VERY ANGRY.
WHAT DID YOU DO, GIRL?
HUH?
NOBARA! NOBARA!
I KNOW YOU'RE THERE, NOBARA!
I'D FOR-GOT-TEN...
COME HOME RIGHT AWAY!! THIS INSTANT!!

CRIMSON FIELD
SHOEI
18
25
SHOOT. WE LOST.
PUNISHMENT FOR BEING LATE: WAXING THE FLOOR
I'M NOT MAKING ENOUGH KILLS WHEN I SPIKE.
AND WE NEED TO LEARN MORE ATTACKS.
BUT FIRST... I NEED MONEY FOR FOOD!
GRRROWL

...SO LONG AS SHE SETS HER SIGHTS HIGH.
ONE MORE!
BENINO
4

HOEI
5
BIG DEAL.
IT'S JUST ONE POINT.
SHE'S NEVER ONCE LOOKED LIKE THAT AT HOME.
SHE'S THE SUCCESSOR TO A TRADITIONAL RYOTEI RESTAURANT, RIGHT?
YES.
IMPOSSIBLE! MAKES ME SHUDDER TO THINK OF IT.
WITH VOLLEYBALL, SHE'S GOT POTENTIAL.
SHE'LL BE EVEN BETTER SOON ENOUGH...

WHAM
TING
THAT WAS HIGH!
IT WENT ABOVE THE BLOCKERS!
YES!

POOM
I GOT IT!
HERE!
ONE MORE!
BENINO
4
...IS NO ACE AT ALL!
JUMP

SIS...
HUF
HUF
NOBARA'S LITTLE SISTER.
SHE WANTED TO SEE THE GAME, SO I BROUGHT HER.
YUI, IT'S NO GOOD!
NOBARA'S BEAT.
AN ACE THAT CAN'T JUMP WHEN TIRED...
DOESN'T MATTER.

HUF
HUF
NUMBER 4!
NUMBER 4!
NO 4
DON'T WORRY ABOUT IT!
WHAT AM I DOING?!
HUF
YEAH ...
THE OTHER TEAM'S BLOCKERS ARE SURPRISINGLY GOOD.
SHE'S NOT GETTING THE BALL THROUGH.
OH. HEH ...
WRONG CLOTHES, WRONG PLACE!
HUH?
WHAT?!
YUSHIN! WHO IS THAT?!
...!
YUSHIN?! WHAT ARE YOU DOING HERE?

I'M THE ACE.
BMP
BAM
YAY!!
WAY TO GO!
OH ...!

I APOLOGIZE FOR BEING LATE.
PLEASE LET US PLAY A GAME!!
DRIP
DRIP
PLEASE FORGIVE US!
IT'S ONLY NATURAL.

SLAP
WHERE'VE YOU BEEN?
YOU MORON!
GO APOLOGIZE TO THE OTHER TEAM!
NOW!
YUI'S ANGRY.
...
YES.
BENINO

HUF
HUF
NOBARA...!
BENINO
4
PLEASE WAIT! I PROMISE THAT...
FORGIVE ME FOR BEING LATE!
HA HA
WHAT? WE'RE LEAVING?
SHOEI 12

HURRY, NOBARA! THE OTHER TEAM IS ALREADY—
SHE'S HERE!
MAD DASH
PUM
PUM
PUM
FWOOSH
... HERE.
AHH
WHAT ARE YOU DOING CHANGING HERE?!
THE BOYS' BASEBALL TEAM IS WATCHING!

COACH, LET'S GO.
YOU'RE THE ONES WHO WANTED THIS GAME SO MUCH.
THAT'S WHY WE AGREED TO COME.
HA HA HA! THAT IS TOO FUNNY!
SHOEI
1
12
6
8
SHOEI
...
YOU'VE BEEN SAYING THAT FOR 20 MINUTES ALREADY.
WE DON'T HAVE ALL DAY TO HUMOR YOU, YOU KNOW.
MURMUR
MURMUR
BENINO
1
BENINO
2
6

LET ME GET THERE IN TIME!
IT STARTS AT NOON.
WHAT'S GOING ON?
WHAT DO YOU MEAN, A PLAYER IS MISSING?
PLEASE!
PLEASE GIVE US ANOTHER 10 MINUTES. OR EVEN 5 MINUTES.
I PROMISE SHE'LL COME.
ANOTHER NO-SHOW, HUH?
YOU GUYS HAVE DONE THIS BEFORE, REMEMBER?
NO! THIS IS DIFFERENT. REALLY.

TALL
BIG
I'M YOUR SISTER'S... FRIEND?
OH, UM.
WH-WHO ARE YOU?
FRIEND? IS THAT RIGHT?
WHAT'S YOUR NAME?
WHAT'S YOUR RELATIONSHIP WITH MY SISTER?
OR... CLASS-MATE?
ANYWAY, I'LL TAKE YOU HOME.
ER... WHERE'D MY SISTER GO?
OH, SHE'S GOT A VOLLEYBALL GAME TODAY.

THANKS, SIS.
WHAT?
YEAH. YOU BETTER HURRY.
SORRY! I'LL LEAVE THE REST TO YOU!
FORGET IT.
ACTUALLY, I CAN'T STAY LONG.
HUH? WHAT AM I SUPPOSED TO DO?

VOOSH
OH NO, IT'S NOBARA.
YOU THERE! QUIT MAKING SOUKA CRY!
HERE COMES THAT HIGH KICK OF HERS.
RUN!
OOH IT'S SADAKO!* IT'S SADAKO! CREEPY!
WHY IS YOUR HAIR SO LONG?
HEY! HEY!
STOP IT.
...
*SADAKO IS A CHARACTER IN THE HORROR MOVIE *RINGU*.
SIS.

UH... UM...
WAIT. WAIT, SOUKA.
FWUMP
WAI—
GO SLEEP IT OFF.
SHE CAME FOR ME!

EXCUSE ME, YOU CAN'T...
MY DAD WILL...
UGH!
WHO'S THAT GRIM GUY?
I DON'T CARE IF YOU'RE SOME POLITICIAN'S SON OR NOT.
WE DON'T HAVE TO KOWTOW TO A PERVERT LIKE YOU!
SEIRYU CAN DO GOOD HONEST BUSINESS ON ITS OWN!
LET'S GO, SOUKA.
OH...YES.

BOTH OF YOU ARE SEIRYU GIRLS?!
OW...
MY FACE!
SIS! LET'S GO HOME!
HURRY!
...SIS...?
...MY DAD!!
AGE 22
I'M GONNA TELL...
YOU'VE PISSED ME OFF!
I HOPE YOU KNOW WHAT THAT MEANS FOR YOUR ESTABLISHMENT!!

GET YOUR HANDS OFF SOUKA, YOU PERVERTED CREEP!
Ow! That hurts!
SHUMP

THIS IS ALL NOBARA'S FAULT!
SHE DOESN'T HELP OUT A BIT AT HOME.
ALL SHE THINKS ABOUT IS VOLLEYBALL!
FWP
HM? I DON'T RECALL SAYING...
...THAT YOU HAD MY PERMISSION TO LEAVE!
WHY ISN'T SHE HERE?!
ARGH!
NO! LET GO OF ME!
NOBARA!

I'M COUNTING ON YOU TO WORK HARD FOR SEIRYU.
I CAN'T DO THIS. I JUST CAN'T.
THIS GUY IS ACTING STRANGE.
B-DMP
I...I'M NOT FEELING WELL.
IS IT OKAY IF I GO HOME NOW?
B-DMP
...
UP CLOSE, YOU'RE AS PRETTY AS A DOLL. KNOW THAT?
DON'T RUIN IT BY TALKING.

THEY WERE ON THE VERGE OF SELLING IT...
...WHEN MY DAD HELPED OUT WITH THE FUNDING.
WE OWE A GREAT DEAL TO HIM.
YES... I'VE HEARD.
THEN I'M SURE YOU UNDERSTAND...
...THAT YOU SHOULDN'T MAKE ME ANGRY.
YOU SEEM LIKE A SMART GIRL. YOU UNDERSTAND, DON'T YOU?
MISS SOUKA...
...YOU'RE THE ONLY ONE I CAN RELY ON NOW.
...

RIGHT AFTER I HELP SOUKA, I'LL BE THERE!
YOU KNOW, DON'T YOU?
THERE WAS A TIME WHEN SEIRYU ALMOST WENT UNDER.
IT TAKES SIX PEOPLE TO HAVE A VOLLEYBALL TEAM.
I'M COMING!
I'LL MAKE IT BY GAME TIME, NO MATTER WHAT!
SLAM
THE KYORAN PRINCE HOTEL!
PLEASE HURRY!

GET IN!
THIS GIRL...

IMPOSSIBLE!
...SHE WON'T LISTEN TO A THING ANYONE ELSE SAYS.
SO RASH...
...AND RECKLESS.
ONCE SHE GETS AN IDEA IN HER HEAD...
HELLO? IT'S ME.
I HATE TO DO THIS TO YOU, BUT SOMETHING CAME UP. I CAN'T MAKE IT TODAY.
SCREECH
SORRY.
NOBARA!
...OH...
...OH WELL.
I'LL MAKE IT UP TO YOU ANOTHER TIME, 'KAY?
THAT'S OKAY. I'LL DO SOME SHOPPING OR SOMETHING BEFORE I HEAD HOME.

UM...
I'LL ASK SOMEONE. I'LL FIGURE IT OUT.
ALL THAT RUNNING AND NO IDEA WHERE SHE'S GOING?!
...
SHE'S IMPOSSIBLE!
...
HUF
HUF
...
AND ANYWAY, ISN'T YOUR GIRLFRIEND WAITING FOR YOU, YUSHIN?
GO ON. DON'T WORRY.
I'LL MAKE SURE TO GET BACK IN TIME FOR THE GAME.
...THERE'S ONLY ONE HOUR LEFT.

DON'T YOU THINK IT'S STRANGE?
HAS NOBARA EVER BEEN LATE FOR PRACTICE BEFORE?
HELP ME, SIS!
HEY! I SAID WAIT UP, NOBARA!
asics
NOW THAT YOU'VE MADE IT TO SHINJUKU...
...I HOPE YOU KNOW WHERE THE HOTEL IS!
HUH?
WHERE... IT IS?

UNBELIEV-ABLE!
SHE KNEW WE WERE GONNA PRACTICE AT 10!
WHAT'S NOBARA THINKING?!
...YOU REALLY THINK SO?
I WOULDN'T BE SURPRISED. SHE WAS PRETTY WORKED UP.
I CAN'T BELIEVE THIS.
IT'S OUR FIRST PRACTICE GAME AS A TEAM.
MAYBE SHE WAS TOO EXCITED TO FALL ASLEEP LAST NIGHT AND THEN ENDED UP OVERSLEEPING.

Crimson Hero

SET 11
THE CRYBABY ACE

Crimson
Hero

YUSHIN ?!
ARGH!
DASH
HELP ME, SIS!
WAIT UP, NOBARA!
asics

SO THE DATE WAS TODAY!
WHAT TIME IS IT RIGHT NOW?!
THE GAME IS AT TWELVE.
A LITTLE AFTER TEN.
WHAT THE HECK ARE YOU GONNA DO?
I PROMISE TO MAKE IT BACK BY GAME TIME!
THAT'S IN LESS THAN TWO HOURS!!

HI THERE! ♡
CHATTER
BEEEEP
CHATTER
BEEEEP
HELLO?
HELLO? SOUKA!
WHAT IS IT?! WHAT HAPPENED?
SHE GOT CUT OFF!

I'M IN THE LOBBY OF THE KYORAN PRINCE HOTEL...
I'VE GOT AN OMIAI DATE TODAY.
MOTHER TOLD ME TO COME, BUT...
KLAK
...BUT I'M...I'M SCARED...
HELP ME—
SIS...

HELLO, CRIMSON DORM!
HE'S SUCH A COLD-HEARTED GUY.
BRRRRRRING
BRRRRRRING
SHUT UP!
BY THE WAY, YUSHIN WON'T BE COMING.
HE SAID HE HAS A DATE TODAY.
...
YOUR SISTER...? I CAN'T UNDERSTAND YOU WHEN YOU'RE CRYING.
...WHAT?
HERE! IT'S FOR ME.
WHAT'S WRONG?!
HELLO? SOUKA?! IT'S NOBARA!
PANG

EVERYONE SAID THEY'LL SHOW UP LATER TO CHEER YOU ON, OKAY?
YEAH, DON'T WORRY.
YOU'RE A WORRYWART, TOMONORI!
I'D BETTER STOP WORRYING ABOUT SOUKA.
I'VE GOT TO FOCUS ON TODAY'S GAME.
AFTER ALL, I'M THE ACE!
HEY! WAIT UP! I'LL GO TO THE STATION WITH YOU!
GOT YOUR UNIFORM?
YUP!
A TOWEL?

DON'T YOU FEEL ANY REMORSE ABOUT WHAT YOU'VE DONE?!
SOUKA IS GOING TO BE A HOSTESS TO OUR GUESTS TODAY IN YOUR PLACE.
DON'T WORRY. I UNDERSTAND.
YOU'RE PRETTY CUTE.
SOUKA!

...HOW SHALL I PUT IT... ONE COULD CALL HIM A PLAYBOY.
THE THING IS, MR. YOKOTA'S SON IS...
THEY'RE CALLING IT AN OMIAI DATE...
...BUT I THINK IT'S NOT MUCH MORE THAN HAVING TEA TOGETHER.
WHEN MISS SOUKA SERVED AS HOSTESS TO THE GUESTS THE OTHER DAY...
...HE TOOK A LIKING TO HER.
AND SOUKA?
WHAT DOES SHE THINK?
BUT I DO FEEL SORRY FOR HER.
WELL, IT'S FOR THE GOOD OF SEIRYU, SO SHE ACCEPTED.
OH, MISS NOBARA. PLEASE DON'T TELL THE MISTRESS ...
...THAT I TOLD YOU THIS.

NOBARA, WE'RE TRYING TO START PRACTICE.
DON'T GET MAD AT ME!
YOU KNOW I HAVE NO SAY IN THEIR AFFAIRS.
...
GASP
OH!
SORRY!
WHEN SEIRYU WAS STRUGGLING IN GRANDMOTHER'S GENERATION...
...IT WAS YOUR MOTHER WHO BROUGHT SEIRYU BACK UP TO WHERE IT IS.
I'M SURE SHE HAS SOME PLAN.
WHAT PLAN?!
WHAT IT COMES DOWN TO IS THAT THE RESTAURANT IS ALWAYS MORE IMPORTANT TO HER THAN HER DAUGHTERS.

NO, IT'S JUST THAT I HEARD SOMETHING ODD.
WHAT?
THE KIND THAT CAN LEAD TO AN ARRANGED MARRIAGE? WITH WHOM?!
THE SON OF SOME POLITICIAN.
I GUESS SEIRYU OWES A DEBT OF GRATITUDE TO THIS MAN.
APPARENTLY SOUKA IS GOING ON AN OMIAI DATE.
WHAT?!
SOUKA IS ONLY A THIRD-YEAR IN JUNIOR HIGH!!
WHAT COULD MOTHER BE THINKING?!

WHAT'S UP, AUNT MOMOKO?
JUST THOUGHT I'D HAND THIS TO YOU BEFORE YOU LEFT.
TAKE IT HOME AND EAT IT.
RUSTLE
OH...!
AUNT MO-MOKO ...!
DON'T BE SO CREEPY. BACK OFF!
SO... HOW IS IT GOING?
GREAT! WE'RE IN GREAT SHAPE!!
HMM...
HUH? SOMETHING WRONG?

FWA! FWA!
ARE YOU BLIND? I'M IN THE MIDDLE OF PRACTICE!
GO GET THEM!
WHAT IS SHE DOING HERE?
MOMOKO IS THE ADVISER FOR THE GIRLS' VOLLEYBALL TEAM.
REALLY?
THAT'S IT FOR THE GIRLS.
SURE... IF I CAN GET OUT OF BED BY THEN.
PLEASE, PLEASE MAKE SURE TO COME!!
HIYA.
OH, NURSE. TOMOR-ROW'S GAME...
...STARTS AT NOON. PLEASE DON'T FORGET TO COME.

GO!!!
CRIMSON FIELD HIGH!!
...AWAIT ME ON THAT COURT!
YUSHIN! OH, GOOD.
YOU CAN BRING ME A PAIR OF SLIPPERS.
I CAN'T GO IN.
!
UNBELIEV-ABLE!
WHERE DO YOU GET OFF SMOKING IN THE GYM?!

WE STARTED WITH NOTHING...
...AND NOW WE ARE PLAYING A GAME.
YES, THERE'S SOMETHING THAT DRAWS ME NEAR.
FRIENDSHIPS...
YUI, LET'S DO *THAT* AGAIN. YOU KNOW!
GONNA CRY AGAIN?
SURE!
N-NO! I'M NOT GONNA CRY!
...AND CHALLENGES...

AND NOBARA...
THANK YOU.
I HAVEN'T THANKED YOU PROPERLY YET.
THE TEAM HERE TODAY...
...WOULDN'T BE HERE IF YOU HADN'T GATHERED US TOGETHER.
WITHOUT YOU, WE ALL WOULD'VE GIVEN UP ON VOLLEYBALL.

WHO ELSE BUT YOU?
asics.
THAT'S IT!
HUH?
LEFT FOUR?! BUT THE ACE PLAYS THE STRONG SIDE.
ME?
IT'S EASY TO PREDICT THAT OUR OPPONENTS TOMORROW WILL TARGET RENA.
OKAY!
WE'VE ALL GOT TO COVER HER AS WELL AS WE CAN.
RENA, IT MIGHT BE TOUGH FOR YOU, BUT DO YOUR BEST.
I WILL! ♡ LITTLE RENA WILL FIGHT TO THE END!

L4	C6	S1
NOBARA	RENA	YUI
R3	C5	L2
TOMOYO	KYOKA	AYAKO

YOU'RE ON A ROLL, NOBARA!
OW!
SMAK
asics
THAT HURT, AYAKO.
YOU DON'T KNOW HOW CRAZY STRONG YOU ARE!
YOU'RE SO AWESOME, NOBARA!
SO ARDENT.
BA-BUMP
GET BACK TO PRACTICE ALREADY!
STOP FAWNING OVER HER.
THWOK
WHAT'S A GIRL TO DO?!
KYAAA! NOBARA!
EVERYONE GATHER UP!
I'M GOING TO ANNOUNCE THE POSITIONS FOR TOMORROW'S GAME!

DOMM
...SOMETHING DRAWS ME NEAR.
SOMETHING HERE ON THIS COURT.

MOTHER MIGHT QUESTION WHY I GO TO THESE LENGTHS.
SHE MIGHT NOT UNDER-STAND ME.
BUT I KNOW FOR CERTAIN...

SO NICE AND WARM.
GLAD TO HEAR IT.
STUDIO BUDE
HEY, HAIBUKI! SHE SAYS IT'S GOOD!
THIS IS REALLY GOOD.
YOU EAT, OKAY? AND DO YOUR BEST AT THE GAME!
THIS WAS MY FIRST TIME FOR BOTH.
...AND NEVER WANTED FOR FOOD.
...I NEVER HAD TO WORRY ABOUT MONEY...
IN THE FIFTEEN YEARS OF MY LIFE...
WE JUST ATE!
DOESN'T IT MAKE YOU KINDA HUNGRY TO WATCH HER EAT?
HA HA
NAH, IT'S JUST YOU.

JUST BE QUIET AND EAT, OKAY?!
DON'T DO THAT!
THAT FOOD COMES OUT OF YOUR DORM FEES!
...
HAIBUKI ...
...I'VE BEEN IGNORING YOU THIS WHOLE TIME, YET...
DASH

HOW DO YOU EXPECT TO BE AN ATHLETE IF YOU'RE NOT GONNA EAT PROPERLY?!
DON'T GET MAD AT ME!
DON'T GET... MAD AT ME.
I'M SO HUNGRY...
...I MIGHT START CRYING.
KLANK
WHAT ARE YOU DOING, HAIBUKI?
I THINK WE CAN COOK SOMETHING UP WITH WHAT WE'VE GOT.
YEAH, GOOD IDEA!
WE COULD AT LEAST MAKE PASTA!

DOING...? I'M EATING DINNER.
I'M NOT SHARING.
ONLY A HARD-BOILED EGG?!
I DON'T WANT IT!
HUH?!
YOU USED YOUR FOOD MONEY FOR CLUB DUES?!
WHY ARE YOU ALWAYS IN SOME KIND OF FIX?
WHY DON'T YOU EVER PLAN AHEAD?!
CALM DOWN, YUSHIN. SOME PEOPLE ARE LIKE THAT!
I DO PLAN!
I GAVE IT PLENTY OF THOUGHT, AND I'M DOING WHAT I THINK IS BEST!
WHAT DID YOU HAVE FOR BREAK-FAST?
BREAD.
LUNCH?
... A BUN WITH JAM.

MITSUBA CLUB
VOL.2
WE HAVE FOUR TO FIVE ASSISTANTS COME IN EVERY MONTH. THEY'RE ALWAYS SUCH CHARACTERS SO IT'S A LOT OF FUN FOR ME. SOMETIMES WE'RE ON SUCH A TIGHT DEADLINE THAT EVERYBODY IS SHORT ON SLEEP, SO WE PLAY WORD GAMES TO KEEP OURSELVES AWAKE.
DASH IT ALL.
DA...
MARIA YAMADA
THIS IS WHAT IT'S LIKE AS WE WORK ON THE MANGA.
C'MON EVERYONE!!
GO, TEAM. GO!!
RECENTLY I'VE NOTICED THAT I START WORKING REALLY FERVENTLY WHEN THINGS GET TIGHT. I GOT ONLY FIVE HOURS OF SLEEP IN TRIPLE DAYS!!
AND CHIRO LIKES TO CHEW ON THE STUFF THAT I'VE WORKED ON SO FURIOUSLY.
NIBBLE
IN MY LAP →
OH! NO!!
STUPID! WHAT HAVE YOU DONE, FOOL CAT?!
DARN IT, YOU'RE SO CUTE!
I LOVE YOU, YOU TROUBLEMAKER!!
I'M A HOPELESS DOTING PARENT.
EXCUSE ME! I'D LIKE ONE SWEET BUN!
EGGS
98¢
12 COUNT/LIMIT 1 PER CUSTOMER
IT'S CHEAPER AT THIS STORE!
I'LL MANAGE SOMEHOW!
...
LONG TIME NO SEE. TOMONORI HERE.
WHAT ARE YOU DOING?

SO LITTLE...
CLUB DUES
10000 YEN
1000 YEN
FINE!
I WON'T RELY ON ANYONE AGAIN.
I'LL MANAGE BY MYSELF SOMEHOW!
BUT I WILL SEND NO MONEY TO A DAUGHTER WHO HAS RUN AWAY FROM HOME!!

I'VE RUN OUT OF SAKE, DAD. MAKE THEM BRING MORE.
FORGIVE ME FOR NOT BEING MORE ATTENTIVE!
SOUKA, PLEASE POUR HIM SOME SAKE.
!
...YES.
YOU'RE PRETTY CUTE.

THANK YOU SO MUCH FOR YOUR KIND PATRONAGE.
NOT AT ALL.
BY THE WAY, MISTRESS, IS THIS GIRL THE ONE RUMORED TO BE THE FUTURE MISTRESS?
NO, SHE'S MY YOUNGER DAUGHTER.
THE ELDEST IS LAZY, I'M AFRAID.
MY NAME IS SOUKA. I THANK YOU FOR COMING TO SEIRYU.
HA HA HA
ARE YOU ENJOYING YOURSELF, MR. YOKOTA?
...
HA HA HA
HEY, TAMOTSU! CAN'T YOU AT LEAST OFFER A GREETING?
BY CONTRAST, MY SON...
PAT
AACK
TO HAVE TWO SPLENDID DAUGHTERS AT YOUR YOUNG AGE! I ENVY YOU.

...I'M JUST DEVOTING ALL MY ENERGY TO THE THING THAT'S MOST IMPORTANT TO ME.
MOTHER, WHAT DID NOBARA SAY?
I'M COUNTING ON YOU TO WORK HARD FOR SEIRYU.
I'LL HAVE NOTHING TO DO WITH A DAUGHTER LIKE THAT!
...YES, MOTHER.
MISS SOUKA...
...YOU'RE THE ONLY ONE I CAN RELY ON NOW.

BEEEEEEP
BEEEEEEEEP
YOU ARE THE ELDEST DAUGHTER, BUT BECAUSE YOU INSIST ON PLAYING AROUND...
...YOUR YOUNGER SISTER SOUKA HAS TO BEAR QUITE A BURDEN!
DON'T YOU FEEL ANY REMORSE ABOUT WHAT YOU HAVE DONE?! REALLY...!
CLICK
I'M NOT JUST PLAYING AROUND.
I'M...
AND I DON'T THINK I DID ANYTHING WRONG!

WHY DON'T YOU COME HOME?
I...CAN'T.
THEN I WON'T BE ABLE TO PLAY VOLLEYBALL!
COME HOME.
NO!
FINE, SUIT YOURSELF!
BUT I WILL SEND NO MONEY TO A DAUGHTER WHO HAS RUN AWAY FROM HOME!!
BLAST
I AM BUSY SO I AM HANGING UP!
SOUKA IS GOING TO BE A HOSTESS TO OUR GUESTS TODAY IN YOUR PLACE.
MISTRESS, MISS SOUKA IS READY.

MOTHER, I...
...I GOT THE VOLLEYBALL CLUB GOING AGAIN.
$50 WILL DO.
I NEED IT FOR THE VOLLEYBALL CLUB. IT'S FOR UNIFORMS.
AND WHAT DOES THAT HAVE TO DO WITH SEIRYU?
MISS NOBARA, YOU HAVE GONE OFF TO DO AS YOU PLEASE.
DON'T YOU THINK IT'S SELFISH TO THINK YOU CAN JUST PICK UP THE PHONE TO GET MONEY?
I... CAN'T RIGHT NOW.
ACK!
CAN'T YOU DIRECT SOME OF THAT PASSION OF YOURS TO SEIRYU?
EVERYONE'S WAITING FOR YOU.

MISTRESS, A TELEPHONE CALL FOR YOU.
FROM THE YOUNG MISTRESS!
PATTER
MISTRESS.
GAK! THAT PLAYBOY SON OF HIS?!
HEY, SHHH!
PATTER
MR. YOKOTA, THE POLITICIAN?
THAT'S RIGHT. HE'S COMING TODAY WITH HIS SON.
SEIRYU...
AT LEAST, THAT'S HOW IT HAS ALWAYS BEEN.
FROM A YOUNG AGE, ALL FIRST-BORN DAUGHTERS WERE SUBJECTED TO RIGOROUS INSTRUCTION ON REFINED BEHAVIOR WHILE ALSO LEARNING HOW TO MANAGE THE BUSINESS.
...AND LOOKED AFTER SEIRYU AS THE MISTRESS.
IN EACH GENERATION, THE OLDEST DAUGHTER INHERITED THE ESTABLISH-MENT...
THIS HIGHLY ESTEEMED RYOTEI HAD BEEN PASSED DOWN THROUGH SIX GENERATIONS.
$100?

THIS IS THE ONE THING I NEVER WANTED TO DO.
BRRRRING
BRRRRING
IT'S BEEN A MONTH AND A HALF SINCE I RAN AWAY FROM HOME.
I HATE HAVING TO APPROACH MOTHER FOR MONEY.
BRRRRING
CLICK
THANK YOU FOR CALLING THE SEIRYU RYOTEI...
I'VE SAID THIS BEFORE, BUT...
...MR. YOKOTA WILL BE COMING TODAY.
MAKE SURE THAT HE IS NOT SLIGHTED IN ANY WAY.
YES, MISTRESS.
WHAT ABOUT PARKING?
WE'VE KEPT THE BEST SPOT OPEN FOR HIM.

A GIRL, HUH?
AREN'T YOU THE STUD!
YOU'RE NOT GOING?
I ALREADY MADE PLANS!
IT'S NONE OF YOUR BUSINESS!
HEY... WHERE'S NOBARA?
I SAW HER BY THE PHONE.
...

YOU OUGHT TO MAKE THE EFFORT TO TALK TO YOUR MOTHER.
...
WHAT? THE GIRLS' PRACTICE GAME IS ON SUNDAY?
THIS SUNDAY?
SHOOT, MAN.
I CAN'T.
YOU SHOULD'VE TOLD ME EARLIER.
YEAH. THAT'S WHY...
...THE GUYS GET THE MORNING OFF.
YOU'LL GO WATCH, WON'T YOU, YUSHIN?

I UNDERSTAND YOUR RELUCTANCE TO ASK FOR HELP AFTER YOU'VE RUN AWAY FROM HOME.
BUT WITH CLUB DUES AND THE OTHER THINGS THAT COME UP...
...DON'T YOU THINK YOU'RE GOING TO KEEP HAVING VOLLEYBALL EXPENSES?
YOUR PAY BARELY COVERS YOUR LIVING EXPENSES.
THERE'S A LIMIT TO HOW MUCH YOU CAN DO ON YOUR OWN.
LISTEN. DON'T COUNT ON ME TO DO ANYTHING ELSE FOR YOU.
IF YOU NEED SOME MONEY TO BE ABLE TO KEEP PLAYING VOLLEYBALL ...
...JUST TELL HER SO.

INFIRMARY
I FEEL IMPATIENT WITH MYSELF.
YOU WANT ADVANCE PAY?
SORRY, BUT I JUST GAVE YOU MONEY THE OTHER DAY.
I'VE GOT LESS THAN HALF LEFT, AND THE REST IS FOR MY FOOD THIS MONTH.
I NEED IT TO PAY FOR MY UNIFORM AND STUFF.
IT'S NOT FAIR TO THE OTHERS IF I CAN'T COME UP WITH MY SHARE.
WHAT CAN I DO? WHAT IF I'M THE ONLY ONE WHO CAN'T PAY MY DUES?
YOUR FAMILY ISN'T HURTING FOR MONEY.
WHY DON'T YOU ASK YOUR MOTHER?
I DON'T WANT TO ASK MOTHER!!

OH, NOTHING.
THINGS IN OUR BRAND-NEW GIRLS VOLLEYBALL CLUB...
...ARE AS ROCKY AS EVER.
EVER SINCE I BROKE DOWN IN TEARS IN FRONT OF EVERYONE...
...AS WE LEARN ABOUT EACH OTHER AND OURSELVES.
NOT KNOWING WHEN TO GIVE IN...
...WE KEEP CLASHING...
...I'VE THOUGHT THAT MAYBE I'M THE ONE WITH THE MOST GROWING TO DO.

CUT IT OUT! PLEASE DON'T FIGHT!!
DID YOU HEAR THAT, YUI?
SHE CALLED ME ANNOYING!!
ANGI
IT'S THE TRUTH!
ANGI
!!
ARE YOU GOING TO CRY AGAIN?
HA HA
!
ROOKIE
NO, I'M NOT GOING TO CRY!
WAAA
I SAID I'M NOT CRYING, RENA!
CALM DOWN.
GRAB
DON'T CRY, NOBARA!
WHAT ARE YOU LAUGHING AT, YUSHIN?
RENA'S GOING TO TRY HARD!

I'M NOT SAYING IT'S TERRIBLE.
IT'LL BE FINE ONCE I MAKE THE TEAM STRONGER.
HEY!
CAFETERIA
I'M SORRY OUR CLUB IS PUNY, WITH NO FANS OR ALUMNI TO COUNT ON.
I HEARD YOU, TOMOYO!
AND TO THINK I THOUGHT YOU WERE PRETTY QUIET.
QUIT ACTING LIKE YOU'RE BEING WRONGED ALL THE TIME.
IT'S ANNOYING.
HA! HA HA HA!
WHAT CONFIDENCE! WOW, I GUESS ELITE ATHLETES ARE DIFFERENT FROM THE REST OF US!

SCRATCH
Crimson Hero

Crimso
Hev

SET 10

MISS NOBARA'S PRIVATE FEELINGS

THAT'S RIGHT. WHAT WE GET FROM THE SCHOOL ISN'T NEARLY ENOUGH.
BLIP
BLIP
...WE'RE LOOKING AT...
BUT WHAT WITH UNIFORMS, WATER, AND OTHER EXPENSES...
I'VE TRIED TO KEEP OUR BUDGET AS SMALL AS POSSIBLE.
HUH? PAY DUES FOR CLUB EXPENSES?!
BLIP
CITIZN
600
THAT'S THE THING WITH BEING IN A PUNY CLUB WITH NO SUPPORT-ERS...
$100 EACH?!
ROOKIE

Crimson
Hero

...BUT SOMEHOW...
BASICALLY, YOU'VE GOT A BUNCH OF PEOPLE WHO HARDLY KNOW EACH OTHER.
THIS HAS NOTHING TO DO WITH HIM...
IN THE FIRST PLACE...
...GOOD TEAMS DON'T JUST HAPPEN OVERNIGHT.
HEY, C'MON! QUIT CRYING!
...I FELT LIKE YUSHIN WOULD LISTEN TO ME.

...YOU'LL BE JUST FINE.
YOU'LL GET BEYOND THIS.

THIS HAS NOTHING TO DO WITH HIM.
BUT YOU'VE REALIZED IT NOW, RIGHT?
YOU REALIZE SHE'S BEEN WORKING HARD.
AND YOU RECOGNIZE THAT MAYBE YOU WEREN'T SO THOUGHTFUL ABOUT THE PEOPLE AROUND YOU.
YOU GET IT NOW, RIGHT?
NOD
IF YOU REGRET WHAT YOU'VE DONE AND KNOW YOU CAN DO BETTER...

AND SHE WAS RIGHT!
A TEAMMATE SAID...
...AS LONG AS I GOT THE CLUB GOING, I DIDN'T CARE ABOUT THE PEOPLE IN IT.
I WAS JUST SO IMPATIENT TO PRACTICE.
FOR A SECOND I EVEN THOUGHT OF RENA AS A NUISANCE!
WHY AM I SHARING...
AND RENA'S BEEN WORKING SO HARD!
SHE'S SUCH A GOOD KID...!
...MY FEELINGS WITH YUSHIN?

...
I...
I WAS SO HAPPY TO FINALLY BE ABLE TO PLAY VOLLEYBALL.
YEAH...
...AND?
I FORMED THE CLUB SO WE COULD PLAY VOLLEYBALL TOGETHER.
BUT I WAS SO FOCUSED ON MY OWN GOALS AND...
...AND I WAS SO HAPPY THAT...
DID SOMEONE TELL YOU OFF OR SOMETHING?

OBLIVIOUS TO THE PEOPLE AROUND ME?
HMM. COULD BE.
TRY LOOKING UP.
OH...
SHE'S LEAVING?
HEY, C'MON! WAIT A SEC!
OKAY, OKAY!
WHAT IS IT? WHAT HAPPENED?
HEY!

HAPPEN TO KNOW WHERE MY PUDDING WENT?
RUMBLE
BEATS ME...
YES! FOUND IT!!
I THOUGHT MAYBE TOMONORI SWIPED IT!
WHOA!
YOU SCARED ME! WHAT IS IT?
UM... AM I A HORRIBLE PERSON?
HUH ...?
WHAAA?
WHAT'S WITH YOU?!
SCRA

...
find out
made a
OH! YOU SURPRISED ME.
STILL UP, HUH?
WHATCHA DOING?
YUSHIN.
KCHK
!
SCRATCH
RUMBLE
WHAT THE HECK?
HUH?!
I GOT ASSIGNED A TON EXTRA FOR SNOOZING IN CLASS.
HOMEWORK.

NOBARA?!
WHY ARE YOU CRYING, NOBARA?!
WHAT WAS I DOING?

SOMETHING'S WRONG WITH RENA!
YUI, WHY DON'T YOU BE THE SETTER?
TOMOYO...
AYAKO... AND HER FEELINGS TOWARD YUI.
WHY CAN'T YOU UNDERSTAND?
KYOKA...
YUI... WITH SO LITTLE TIME LEFT BEFORE SHE GRADUATES.
HOW COULD I FORGET ABOUT YOU, RENA?!
WHY WOULD YOU SAY THAT?!
THEY'RE ALL MY TEAMMATES!!

...DON'T FORGET ABOUT ME, OKAY?
KNOW WHAT, NOBARA?
YOU DON'T ACTUALLY CARE ABOUT THE PEOPLE!
I...I WANT TO PRACTICE WITH YOU TOO, NOBARA!
TMP
RENA... ALWAYS DOING DRILLS BY HERSELF IN THE CORNER OF THE GYM.

WHY WAS I SO DENSE?!
NOBARA?
RENA! ARE YOU OKAY?
YOU DON'T HAVE TO GET UP.
I'M FINE.
HEE HEE. SHE SAID IT'S JUST STIFF MUSCLES.
HOW EMBAR-RASSING.
...
NOBARA...
I'M GOING TO WORK SUPER HARD SO I CAN PLAY WITH THE REST OF YOU AS SOON AS POSSIBLE.
SO... SO UNTIL THEN...

ZWP
STIFF MUSCLES THROUGH HER WHOLE BODY!
SHE'S RUNNING A FEVER, TOO. WHAT DID YOU DO TO HER?
FOOTWORK DRILLS AND MUSCLE-BUILDING.
I WAS TRYING TO BUILD UP HER STRENGTH.
WELL, LISTEN UP. MUSCLES ARE SOMETHING YOU BUILD UP GRADUALLY.
SUDDEN RIGOROUS EXERCISE IS DANGEROUS AND COUNTER-PRODUCTIVE.
...
I'M SORRY. IT'S MY FAULT.
...
CLAMP
RENA MUST'VE BEEN FEELING BAD...
STOP IT! DON'T CLING TO ME DURING PRACTICE!

YUI, WHY DON'T YOU BE THE SETTER?
I CAN PLAY ANY POSITION.
HEY!!
UM...
...SOMETHING'S WRONG WITH RENA!
RENA...!
INFIRMARY

YUI, I WANT TO HIT OFF YOUR TOSS!
I DON'T THINK WINNING IS EVERY-THING.
I DON'T CARE IF I'M STRONG OR NOT.
WELL, I DON'T.
...WHY CAN'T YOU UNDERSTAND?
YUI!
IT'S NOT MUCH LONGER...
...THAT I GET TO PLAY VOLLEYBALL WITH YOU.
WHY...

CAN'T YOU JUST TRY IT?
WHY DON'T WE JUST LISTEN TO WHAT YUI SAYS? SHE'S THE CAPTAIN.
KNOW WHAT, NOBARA? YOU ONLY CARE ABOUT HAVING A CLUB.
YOU DON'T ACTUALLY CARE ABOUT THE PEOPLE IN IT!
YOU THINK BEING A STRONG PLAYER IS ALL THAT MATTERS?

clamp
I JUST WANT TO HURRY UP AND PRACTICE.
NOBARA?
I'VE BEEN HITTING OFF YOUR TOSS SINCE MY FIRST YEAR HERE.
WHAT, RENA?
YOU'LL BE FINE. YOU SAW HER TECHNIQUE, DIDN'T YOU?
...
RENA?
THIS AGAIN?!
STOP IT! DON'T CLING TO ME DURING PRACTICE!

asics.
SHE'S THE SETTER FOR THIS NEXT GAME.
TRUE. YOU AND TOMOYO ...
...NEED TO WORK SOME OUT.
BUT ...
YUI! YOU'RE THE SETTER!
WITH TOMOYO AS THE SETTER...
I CAN'T HIT OFF HER!
...WE'LL HAVE A WIDER VARIETY OF ATTACKS TO USE.

*COMBINATIONS ARE ATTACKS COORDINATED BETWEEN THE SETTER AND THE ATTACKER.

AND I'M NOT GOING TO BE OUTDONE BY YOUR BELOVED NOBARA SUMIYOSHI!
N-NOBARA?
NOBARA!
...RATHER THEN BEING LADYLIKE...
WH-WHAT'S SO FUNNY?!
NOTHING. I WAS JUST THINKING HOW CUTE YOU ARE, TOMOYO.
WHAT?
YOU SMART ALECK!
...I PREFER PLAYING VOLLEYBALL. THAT'S ALL I NEED TO BE HAPPY.
RATHER THAN CHASING AFTER LOVE...

AND IT WASN'T BECAUSE NOBARA SUMIYOSHI ASKED ME TO EITHER!
YOU DID IT FOR YOURSELF, RIGHT?
THAT'S REASON ENOUGH, ISN'T IT?
...
YOU'VE GOT TO DECIDE FOR YOURSELF WHAT YOU'RE WORTH!
YES. I'M GOING TO PLAY VOLLEYBALL AGAIN...
...TO SEE WHAT I CAN MAKE OF MYSELF.

LATER...
SEE YA...
...I DON'T EVEN KNOW WHAT IT FEELS LIKE...
SO... WAS YOUR KNEE ALRIGHT?
YES.
JUST SO IT'S CLEAR, I DIDN'T JOIN VOLLEYBALL BECAUSE YOU TOLD ME TO DO IT.
OKAY.
...TO LIKE SOMEBODY IN THAT WAY.

SWISH
HAIBUKI!
TAKE THOSE TO THE TRAINING ROOM.
OH, RIGHT.
...
I HAVEN'T SPOKEN TO HAIBUKI SINCE THAT NIGHT.
I TRY NOT TO MEET HIS GAZE AT THE DORM, EITHER.
I BROKE UP WITH TOMOYO...
...BECAUSE I COULDN'T GET YOU OUT OF MY MIND, NOBARA.
I...

I HAVE TO GO COOK DINNER FOR THE DORM.
SHE'S JUST TEACHING YOU THE BASICS.
KEEP IT UP.
NOBARA, MY ARMS HURT.
WBBL
SO DO MY LEGS. AND TOMOYO SCARES ME.
NOBA—
SHOOT! THE TIME!
SORRY! GOTTA RUN!
...
SLAM
GIRLS' LOCKER R
asics
UNIFORMS
NOBODY
MOVE
DIDN

GOOD WORK, EVERYONE!!
TAP
TAP
NOT FAST ENOUGH.
WHAT ARE YOU DOING? TIRED ALREADY?
TWEET
NOT LIKE THAT. TAKE WIDER STEPS!
TWEET
TWEET

OOH, YOU'RE A DEMON COACH!!
Y-YES!!
...AT LEAST LEARN THE RULES AND ETIQUETTE!
GET A LOAD OF TOMOYO.
YOU MAKING FUN OF ME?
WHAT?
N-NO.
SHE ACTS LIKE SHE'S SO GREAT.
YEAH, BUT YOU'VE GOTTA ADMIT SHE'S GOOD.
IT WAS SO EASY TO HIT OFF HER!
asics.

THWOK
...
HMPH
IS SOMEONE GOING TO TRAIN HER, OR WHAT?
YOU DON'T EXPECT US TO PRACTICE WITH A BEGINNER WHO DOESN'T EVEN KNOW HOW TO MOVE, DO YOU?
RENA, IF YOU WANT TO PRACTICE WITH THE REST OF US...
IF YOU'D LIKE, I'LL TEACH HER—STARTING WITH THE BASICS.
AFTER ALL, WHEN GAME-TIME COMES WE'LL NEED HER TO PLAY.
OH... YOU'RE RIGHT.
I'D FORGOTTEN.

SLAM
SOK
THE NEW CRIMSON FIELD HIGH GIRLS' VOLLEYBALL CLUB!!
!
HUFF
W-WATCH IT...
TEE HEE
I...I WANT TO PRACTICE WITH YOU TOO, NOBARA! ♡
RENA KOMIZO, FIRST-YEAR

HEY KYOKA, YOU'RE GOOD!!
ACTUALLY, I WAS A STARTER IN JUNIOR HIGH.
OH, THANKS.
YES! WE CAN PULL THIS OFF.
WITH THESE PLAYERS...
BA-BUMP
...WE MIGHT BE ABLE TO WIN AT LEAST ONE GAME AT THE REGIONAL PRELIMS!
BA-BUMP
...THAT NEVER WON A SINGLE GAME?
LOOK AT US!
THE GIRLS HAVE A LOT OF SPIRIT!
WHAT'S GOING ON? IS THAT REALLY THE TEAM...
THEY'RE PRACTICING HARD EVEN WITH THE HIGH NET.
AND DID YOU SEE THE SETTER WITH THE LONG HAIR?

WE'VE NEVER PLAYED TOGETHER BEFORE...
BA-BUMP
...
THE BALL CAME TO ME AS IF MY HAND WAS DRAWING IT IN.
YOU THINK SO?
I THINK YOU'RE BETTER, YUI.
AYAKO MOCHIDA, SECOND-YEAR
...BUT SHE KNOWS...
BA-BUMP
...EXACTLY WHERE IT'S EASIEST FOR ME TO HIT!
POM
KYOKA GOTO, FIRST-YEAR

BAM
I CAN FINALLY PLAY...
SHOK
TOMOYO OSAKA, SECOND-YEAR
SEE THAT? TOMOYO IS AMAZING!
YOU CAN'T TELL AT ALL THAT SHE HASN'T PLAYED FOR TWO YEARS!
YUI SUZUSHIRO, THIRD-YEAR CAPTAIN OF THE GIRLS' CLUB
asics
asics

I DON'T WANT TO WASTE TIME.
LET'S HURRY UP AND START PRACTICE.
I DON'T CARE IF WE'RE OFF IN THE CORNER OF THE GYM.
I DON'T CARE IF WE DON'T HAVE MUCH SPACE.
BECAUSE FINALLY...
SQUEEK
...
...FINALLY... I CAN PLAY VOLLEYBALL.

CLAP CLAP
...
MAYBE YOU CAN, BUT...
STUPID ...
THAT WAS GREAT, NOBARA!
DON'T EVER INTERFERE WHEN THE GUYS ARE PRACTICING!
AS OF TODAY, THE GIRLS' CLUB IS OFFICIALLY IN ACTION!
...
R R R R
HEH
AS USUAL, SHE NEVER DOES THINGS THE NORMAL WAY!

OOF!
THOK
!
GAK!!
BOK
YUI! IT'S OKAY!!
WE CAN STILL HIT IT OVER AT THE GUYS' HEIGHT!!
NOBARA SUMIYOSHI, FIRST-YEAR, GIRLS' VOLLEYBALL CLUB

MITSUBA CLUB
Vol. 1
OUR CHIEF ASSISTANT MAKES OUR LUNCHES AT WORK AND LET ME TELL YOU—THEY ARE GOOD.
WE HAVE A SCHEDULE FOR EACH MONTH THAT'S CRAMMED WITH DETAILS ABOUT HOW MY WORK SHOULD BE PROGRESSING AND WHAT THE ASSISTANTS' SCHEDULES ARE. AT THE BOTTOM IT ALSO SHOWS WHAT EACH DAY'S MENU WILL BE. IT ACTUALLY TAKES ABOUT TEN DAYS TO GET THE PAGES DONE, BUT IT'S A HUGE UNDERTAKING TO GO GROCERY SHOPPING FOR TEN DAYS' WORTH OF FOOD. AT FIRST I WENT ALONG TOO, BUT THESE DAYS I JUST LEAVE IT TO HER. SHE HAULS BACK ABOUT TWO CARDBOARD BOXES WORTH OF FOOD IN A CART.
IT'S SO MUCH FOOD THAT EVEN THE SUPERMARKET CLERKS GET SURPRISED EVERY TIME.
HOW EM-BAR-RASS-ING!
THE CASHIER RECOGNIZES ME NOW!
CHIEF
BUY A CAR!
SHE MAKES COMMENTS LIKE THIS, BUT EVERY MONTH SHE TURNS A HUGE QUANTITY OF GROCERIES INTO DELICIOUS MEALS. I'M GRATEFUL TO HER.
YUM!
YUM!
SALMON ANKAKE
BY THE WAY, EVERY MONTH WE GO THROUGH A TUBE OF MAYONNAISE. S-SCARY!
THERE ARE ONLY SIX OF YOU!
IF YOU COMPLAIN, I'LL BE PISSED OFF.
UH-HUH...
HE'S ALREADY PISSED OFF.
SOME GUYS NEVER GET TO DO ANYTHING BUT FETCH BALLS, EVEN THOUGH THEY'D LOVE TO PRACTICE!
YEAH, WELL, WE'RE A BIG GROUP WITH 32 MEMBERS!
TWEET
NEXT!
TWEET
HUH?
DASH
HEY!

BA
M
CHECKMATE... ♡
NO WAY!
WE CAN ONLY USE HALF A COURT?!
WE REGISTERED, AND NOW WE'RE AN OFFICIAL CLUB!!
IT'S NOT FAIR!
HOW ARE WE SUPPOSED TO PRACTICE ON HALF A COURT?
AND THE NET IS SET AT THE GUYS' HEIGHT, TOO!
WE CAN CHANGE THE HEIGHT HALFWAY THROUGH PRACTICE.
BOYS' VOLLEYBALL SPACE
GIRLS' VOLLEY-BALL SPACE
TWO COURTS
GYM #1
...
TAKAHASHI, CAPTAIN OF THE BOYS' VOLLEYBALL TEAM
HEY, THAT'S ALREADY A BIG CONCESSION.

IF THERE'S EVER ANYTHING I CAN DO TO HELP YOU...
REALLY! THE THINGS I HAVE TO DO FOR NOBARA!
I DON'T KNOW ABOUT THAT.
NOD
AH. I SEE.
NOD
THE STUDENTS TRUST YOU, NURSE MOMOKO!!
NURSE MOMOKO!!
C'MON!
OH YEAH!
FAMOUS COOKIES OF NAGASHIMA
BONK
AH!
KLAK
THANK YOU, PRINCIPAL.
I'LL BE SURE TO LET YOU KNOW...!
THE NEWLY APPOINTED ADVISER TO THE GIRLS' VOLLEYBALL CLUB

KLAK
THE ADVISER FOR THE GIRLS' VOLLEYBALL CLUB?!
YES.
KLAK
INFIRMARY
OH?
WELCOME TO THE CRIMSON FIELD HIGH GIRLS' VOLLEYBALL CLUB!
I'M ALSO FILLING IN AS A DORM MOTHER...
...I'M REALLY QUITE BUSY...
...BUT THE STUDENTS BEGGED ME.
MOMOKO SUMIYOSHI, SCHOOL NURSE, CRIMSON FIELD HIGH SCHOOL

WITHOUT BATTING AN EYE...
...OUR FINAL MEMBER SUBMITTED HER NAME.
YOU'VE GOT TO DECIDE FOR YOURSELF WHAT YOU'RE WORTH!
I DON'T KNOW WHAT CAUSED HER CHANGE OF HEART...
CLASS REGISTRATION TOMOKO OSAKA GIRLS' VOLLEYBALL
...BUT...
...I HAD A HUNCH.

THE MAKING OF CRIMSON HERO

HI EVERYONE! HERE'S VOLUME 3. HOW HAVE YOU ALL BEEN?

AS USUAL I'VE BEEN BUSY ALL THE TIME, BUT THE OTHER DAY I GOT TO GO SEE THE TOKYO PRELIMINARIES FOR THE SPRING HIGH SCHOOL VOLLEYBALL TOURNAMENT. (I WENT A YEAR AGO...HOW QUICKLY A YEAR PASSES!) ANYWAY, ONCE AGAIN IT REALLY MOVED ME. YOU KNOW WHY? BEFORE THE PLAYERS ENTERED THE COURT, THEY WERE STANDING IN A ROW HOLDING HANDS!!! OH THOSE HIGH SCHOOL GIRLS, JUST BEFORE THE GAME!!!!

AND IT JUST SO HAPPENED THAT THIS TEAM WAS FROM A VOLLEYBALL CLUB WITH ONLY SIX MEMBERS!

DANGER, DANGER! I'VE SUCCUMBED AGAIN!!

THESE COMIC PAGES WILL COME OUT IN MARCH, AND THAT'S RIGHT SMACK DURING THE SPRING TOURNAMENT. I WANT TO GO EVERY DAY, SO I'VE ALREADY STARTED CRAMMING ON MY WORK. I'M GOING TO GO NO MATTER WHAT! (I'M WAY BEHIND.)

THIS YEAR FOR SURE!! THIS YEAR FOR SURE I'LL HAVE A CAMERA THAT'S NOT BROKEN!!!!

IF YOU SEE A STRANGE WOMAN CRYING HER EYES OUT AT YOYOGI, PLEASE LOOK UPON HER KINDLY.

SHE'S CRYING AGAIN!!

MITSUBA
TAKANASHI
SET 9
THE NEW CRIMSON
FIELD HIGH GIRLS'
VOLLEYBALL CLUB
Crimson
Hero

CONTENTS

Set 9
The New Crimson Field High Girls' Volleyball Club
3

Set 10
Miss Nobara's Private Feelings
45

Set 11
The Crybaby Ace
91

Set 12
Silent Love
137

STORY THUS FAR

Nobara Sumiyoshi is a first-year high school student who lives for her one passion, volleyball. She's the successor to Seiryu, the high-class ryotei restaurant that her family runs, but she enrolled in Crimson Field High School expressly to play volleyball. Her mother pulled strings and eliminated the girls' volleyball club before Nobara started her first day of school there. Furious, Nobara ran away from home. While living and working in the Crimson Dorm, a dorm for boys' volleyball scholarship students, she began assembling a girls' volleyball club. Enduring harassment from members of the boys' club, she worked hard until she was only one member short of a full team.

That's when she met Tomoyo Osaka, a former member of the Japan Junior Youth team. Nobara wanted her to join, but Tomoyo refused. Unable to overcome a setback after being injured, Tomoyo had already given up on volleyball. Finally, Nobara told her bluntly, "You've got to decide for yourself what you're worth!"

Albany County Public Library
Laramie, WY
Where your books came from in 2005-2006:

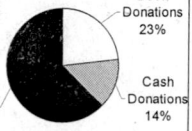

Crimson Hero™

Story & Art by
MITSUBA TAKANASHI